Anolis carolinensis, the common green anole. Two specimens or even more can be kept in one cage if it is large enough and the specimens are all about the same size. Be sure they all get the chance to eat and drink enough. Photo by G. Marcuse.

This Jamaican giant anole, *Anolis garmani,* was photographed in Miami. Adults grow to 18 inches in length and will eat small mice and birds. Photo by J. Bridges courtesy "The Shed" of Miami, Florida.

CONTENTS

Title Page: *Chamaeleo* sp., possibly *C. hoehnelii.* Photo by G. Marcuse.

ISBN 0-87666-772-8

Distributed in the U.S. by T.F.H. Publications, Inc., 211 West Sylvania Avenue, PO Box 427, Neptune, NJ 07753; in England by T.F.H. (Gt. Britain) Ltd., 13 Nutley Lane, Reigate, Surrey; in Canada to the pet trade by Rolf C. Hagen Ltd., 3225 Sartelon Street, Montreal 382, Quebec; in Canada to the book trade by H & L Pet Supplies, Inc., 27 Kingston Crescent, Kitchener, Ontario N28 2T6; in Southeast Asia by Y.W. Ong, 9 Lorong 36 Geylang, Singapore 14; in Australia and the South Pacific by Pet Imports Pty. Ltd., P.O. Box 149, Brookvale 2100, N.S.W. Australia; in South Africa by Valid Agencies, P.O. Box 51901, Randburg 2125 South Africa. Published by T.F.H. Publications, Inc., Ltd., the British Crown Colony of Hong Kong.

ameleons
and anoles

by mervin f. roberts

This fine *Anolis equestris* or knight anole was taken from an "immigrant" colony near Miami. Its colors are exceptionally bright because it is just finishing the molt. Although a bit thin, a few cockroaches or crickets each day would soon bring it to the peak of plumpness. Photos by J. Dommers courtesy "The Shed" of Miami, Florida.

Green anoles, both fine specimens. Photos by J. Dommers.

Acknowledgments

My daughter Martha spent many hours in Kline Library at Yale University and the U.S. National Museum Library Index in Washington on the literature search. My wife, Edith, patiently typed from handwritten scribbles which I wrote but later could hardly decipher. My publisher, Dr. Herbert R. Axelrod, waited nearly two years for something which we all thought should have been done in just a few months. Professor Lewis D. Ober of Miami-Dade Community College graciously gave me advice and counsel. John Dommers and Jim Bridges made color photographs especially for this book. My daughter Nancy stuck with me during a tiring and difficult trip to Florida to learn about the "Immigrants," and Louis Porras of Miami provided some of the material for the photographs. I enjoyed every minute and hope some of it rubs off.

Mervin F. Roberts
Old Lyme, Connecticut

Introducing Anoles and Chameleons

In books of this sort it is important for the readers and the author to agree on *what* the book is "All About." For anyone who does not already know an anole from a chameleon, this would be difficult, were it not for the pictures. For the moment, then, this is a book about keeping captive the lizards which appear in the pictures. To use the words of a standard authority does not help much. *Webster's Unabridged Dictionary*, Second Edition, starts off beautifully with an excellent description of a chameleon but then goes on to muddy the waters. The dictionary tells us that the name derives from the French *chame* = dwarf, and *leon* = lion. Be grateful that Noah was not a Frenchman. The dictionary goes on to state that: "From its power of living for long periods without food, the chameleon was formerly supposed to feed upon air." Unfortunately, this part of that description is lethally wrong. Chameleons cannot live for long periods without food. Deprived of food and water they will not live as long as most turtles or toads under the same conditions. As a matter of fact, chameleons are voracious feeders. A second problem is with the anole part of the title of this book. Here it is confusing because the uninformed public calls anole lizards "chameleons," this because they can change color dramatically

Anolis equestris devouring a grasshopper. The larger anoles can make quick work of even large active insects. Photos by J. Dommers courtesy "The Shed" of Miami, Florida.

The knight anole shown here is probably an older adult. Notice the long white stripe over the shoulder, a sure sign of the species. Photos by G. Marcuse.

much in the same manner as the true chameleons.

Some people believe that chameleons and anoles live on sugar water. This is not true either, but at least these creatures will not die of thirst, they will just starve to death. The truth is that anoles and chameleons require large quantities of water and are predatory insect-eating lizards. They are big eaters, and when they don't eat (or don't eat enough) they use up their stored fat and glycogen; when that is gone, they die of starvation. Some anoles will supplement their diet with fruits and other vegetation, but these seem to be second-choice food. More about that later.

The dictionaries also point out that both chameleons and anoles are distinguished by their ability to change color. This is true but not at all exclusive with these animals. Geckos, some other lizards, many fishes, and certain tree frogs can change their color rapidly and dramatically.

So, simply stated, this is a book for pet keepers about those lizards which are *commonly* called "chameleons." Some are from the New World, and these are more properly called "anoles." All the others are from the Old World, and they are the "*true* chameleons." Taxonomically, they are not closely related. The words anole and chameleon will never be used interchangeably in this book.

One species of chameleon comes from the Mediterranean regions and another is found in India and Ceylon. Half the remaining species are native to Madagascar, and the other half are African.

The anoles are centered in the Caribbean Islands and the adjacent mainland. Only one species is native north of Florida, and only a very few are native to northern South America. Thanks to small boys and banana boats there are thriving populations of anoles in localities where they are not native. For example, at least two species of Cuban anoles are found in the Florida Keys, Miami, and Tampa.

Apart from their natural ranges, the outstanding differences are that anoles have long straight, flexible, non-prehensile tapering tails which break off under stress, and they have narrow heads and short tongues. Chameleons have well-fixed tails which are generally prehensile and are rarely completely straightened. Anoles are long slender animals. They dash about at high speed and are prone to jump. Chameleons are flat, slow, and compacted from side to side. They look like grotesque leaves sitting on edge. They have large heads, swivel eyes, and about the longest tongues, relative to their body length, in the animal kingdom. They do *not* look like dwarf lions.

As is customary with books in this TFH series, the "tree of life" will be laid out, but in this instance there will be a branching at the family level where we separate the Old World chameleons from the New World anoles.

Kingdom Animalia — Animals, not including plants and other lower forms of life.

Phylum Chordata — Chordates, with dorsally located central nervous systems or "spinal cords." This eliminates mollusks, worms, insects, etc.

Class Reptilia — Cold-blooded, with lungs, born on

Two seldom seen anoles. Above, *Anolis roquet aeneus;* below, *Anolis homolechis.* Photos by R.G. Tuck, Jr., courtesy U.S. National Museum.

Anolis sagrei has a well defined pattern of chevrons which are visible even in pale specimens (below). Dark specimens which are molting or recently molted have the pattern much more distinct (above). Photos by J. Dommers.

land. Eliminating fish, amphibians, birds, and mammals.

Order Squamata — Scaly reptiles, not including crocodiles and turtles.

Suborder Sauria — Just lizards; also called Lacertilia.

Family Iguanidae — The genus of anoles is here with some fifty other genera as well.

Family Chamaeleonidae — The true chameleons are here alone. There are three genera.

The family Iguanidae includes nearly all the New World arboreal lizards, about fifty genera with nearly 350 species. The genus *Anolis*, from whence comes the popular pet species *A. carolinensis*, encompasses 100 or so species (or if you count subspecies, say 300) of small lizards that move rapidly, eat insects and change color.

The other family of lizards discussed in this book is the Chamaeleonidae. These are the Old World true chameleons. Depending on whose book you are reading, there are two or three genera. In this book there will be three.

Chamaeleo — About eighty species from Africa, Madagascar, Arabia, Spain, India and Ceylon. Prehensile tails. Some species have been assigned to *Lophosaura* and others to *Microsaura* by taxonomists.

Brookesia — Three species from Madagascar. Their tails are relatively short and not prehensile.

Rhampholeon — One or perhaps two species in this genus from tropical Africa. Tails like *Brookesia*. Some taxonomists drop this genus and place its species elsewhere.

Readers may become annoyed as they look for hard facts and are presented instead with "or so" and "perhaps." This book is not an attempt by a systematist or a taxonomist to classify lizards, but rather it is intended to present their natural history in such a manner as to make pet keeping more successful, humane, and rewarding. The animals we are studying here sometimes vary very slightly. The shape or number of scales between their eyes, the number of teeth, the relative length of their legs, and the arrangement of their chromosomes are some factors which determine what is a species, subspecies, or a race. Also, names change because new information is being constantly added to our fund of knowledge. New specimens are captured and examined, old specimens are re-examined with new instruments, the fossil record is being expanded constantly, and experts are human—sometimes they change their minds.

A few examples should suffice to make this point. Raymond L. Ditmars, in his classic *Reptiles of the World* (New York, Macmillan, 1933) says on page 41 that there are: 44 species in the genus *Chamaeleo,* 3 *Brookesia*, and 2 *Rhampholeon*, for a total of 49. Then on page 111 of the *very same book* he tells us about 45 species of *Chamaeleo,* 3 *Brookesia*, and 2 *Rhampholeon*, for a total of *50* species. His book was first published in 1910 and then revised through the years. Analysis of the 1933 edition suggests that another species of the genus *Chamaeleo* was described and classified sometime between 1910 and 1933.

To carry this one step further, another classic in the field of popular natural history books is the *Larousse Encyclopedia of Animal Life* (New

The European chameleon, *Chamaeleo chamaeleon,* includes both extreme southern Europe and northern Africa in its range. Above, the tongue is brought into play in capturing an insect. Below, a defensive pose. Photo above by G. Marcuse, that below by H. Hansen, Aquarium Berlin.

Corythophanes cristatus lives in trees in Honduras and other Central American areas. Although not an anole, it is another type of iguanid specialized for an arboreal existence. Photo by J. Bridges.

Green anoles are familiar pets which adapt well to captivity and gentle handling. Photo by J. Dommers.

York, McGraw Hill, 1967). This book states on page 311: "There are over eighty species of chameleons occurring mainly in Africa and Madagascar."

The latest edition of the *Encyclopedia Britannica* tells us that there are 84 species of chameleons: *Chamaeleo* is represented by 68 species and *Brookesia* is represented by 16 species. *Rhampholeon* is not mentioned; the expert who wrote that article considers this genus to be invalid, and he may very well be right.

Most of us like animals to have names. One problem is how to get everyone concerned to agree on who does the naming (easy) and how it is done (much less easy). Then the next problem is to use the names universally with the animals to which they have been applied. The definitions are as exact as man knows how to define things, but the interpretations of what is observed vary with the interpreter and the observer (not often the same person). Now this work of necessity requires highly informed opinion, and this leads to highly opinionated information. Optimists with the long view say that this is how mankind upgrades knowledge and conditions of life.

Some pet keepers are apt to be irritated because "the books keep changing the names and the rules." Yes, this is true. It is also true that when this author was a boy he had to eat spinach at least three times a week to retain his health, and in 1943 nearly everyone who made decisions told everyone else that DDT was the panacea for all the ills that insects plague us with. These turned out to be less than true. About the same time most of us brushed our teeth by scrubbing the brush across them. Then in 1960 or so we were

This attractive European chameleon displays most of the features which make the family easy to recognize—the eye in a movable turret, two toes with a common base on the front feet and three on the hind, and a prehensile tail. Photo by L.E. Perkins.

Chamaeleo jacksoni. A mature male with fully developed horns.
Photo by J. Bridges.

Color variation in *Chamaeleo chamaeleon* is common. Photo by J. Bridges.

Chamaleo parsonii is relatively smooth-skinned for a chameleon and has an attractive color pattern. Notice the molting skin on the forelegs. Photo by Dr. O. Klee.

instructed by our dentists that we should not do that, but should scrub up and down rather than across. Now as this book is written the order from the author's dentist is to scrub across but not up and down. When the dentist's children come to the herpetologist and ask "Why do the books keep changing the names?", what shall we tell them?

Try this:

1) We have new tools for research now. We are able to microscopically examine the chromosomes within a cell and count and classify these chromosomes by shape and number. This literally separates the sheep from the goats since it is not possible to produce viable fertile offspring which resemble their parents from sex cells which are not similarly arranged.

2) We have new fossil information which helps scholars to follow lines of evolutionary change. Sometimes a "missing link" is unearthed which demonstrates a relationship never before anticipated or solidly proven.

3) We have new specimens and re-examinations of old specimens which add to our fund of knowledge and again demonstrate relationships which were not previously recognized.

4) We have new tools for data manipulation. The computer is such a tool and with it, for example, chromosome numbers and arrangements can be catalogued and examined readily. Another tool is the instant copy machine which makes inexpensive and exact reproductions of existing information available to everyone. Within the memory of this author the only practical and economical way to see a passage from a rare textbook was to visit the library where the book was kept and read it there. Now through the copy machines, reprints

are readily available from practically anywhere and at low cost. The computer also aids in such important but time consuming projects as creating indices alphabetically by subject and then alphabetically by author or any other criterion. This sort of labor-saving gives scientists more time for study as it relieves them of this tedium.

5) We certainly have more well educated, and perhaps more opinionated, people who are interested and are contributing to our fund of knowledge.

So the names change.

Dr. Herndon G. Dowling is a herpetologist who has made a long and thoughtful study of reptiles and their relationships. In the 1974 *Yearbook of Herpetology* which he edited, he sums it up in two sentences. "A taxonomic classification is not a revelation of eternal reality, to be engraved in stone, but merely the reflection, in formal and abbreviated style, of the current state of knowledge about the relationships of a group of organisms. Often it reflects only the knowledge and prejudice of a single individual."

Not wishing to belabor the point further, this book will concern itself with the natural history, care, health, feeding, reproduction, longevity and habits of anoles and chameleons. The photographs should help with identification since they were chosen to display the prominent and recognizable features of the species most frequently encountered in the lists and the shops of the dealers.

Pet keepers who have had experience with small lizards will understand why this book combines the family of chameleons with the genus of anoles. They do have much in common. One or two specimens of most species can be housed in a

Chamaeleo melleri in a typical chameleon pose. Notice that the eye is looking backward. Photo by H. Hansen, Aquarium Berlin.

Right: Mature female. Note the lack of horns and the shape of the crest. **Below:** Day-old baby. The tiny horn buds show that it is a male. Photos by J. Bridges.

ten-gallon capacity aquarium or a cage of that size. Both chameleons and anoles eat insects. Larger species of both are known to eat small birds and small mice. Both are active in daylight and quiet at night. Both are mostly arboreal, some descending only to lay their eggs. Both are represented by species which are readily available and attractive as caged pets. Both are represented by species which can make dramatic color changes. And both are sometimes blessed with the same common name—chameleon.

For readers who wish to read more and in more detail, a few words are in order. There is no formal bibliography here, but the selected list of references includes useful material for both anoles and chameleons. Anoles and chameleons have been extensively studied, and any of the papers referred to here will also lead to additional information. The only problem one might encounter is that of obtaining copies or reprints of some of the less commonly circulated bulletins and reports. The best sources are the libraries of the large universities and natural history museums. For example, in the northeastern U.S. the libraries of the U.S. National Museum, Washington, D.C., the Museum of Natural History in New York, Kline Library at Yale University, New Haven, and the Library of the Museum of Comparative Zoology at Harvard College, Cambridge, Massachusetts have all or most of the literature referenced in this book. Many provide reprint service at reasonable prices. Not all are open to the public, and you should write first and tell them what you are after.

Natural History of Anoles

To simplify the reading (and the writing) of this book, the natural histories of the two groups will be considered separately. A few aspects which they do have in common will be mentioned as they come up—color is one such.

For most North American and many European pet keepers, the first and possibly the only anole they get to see is *Anolis carolinensis*. The unscientific names of this seven-inch lizard are anole, anolis, green anole, and incorrectly but nevertheless "chameleon." Its natural range is from southeastern Virginia to the Florida Keys and westward to eastern Texas. Other introduced species in the genus overlap this one in Florida and are distributed all over the Caribbean Islands and the adjacent mainland.

The anoles are arboreal, egg laying, agile, predatory lizards. The smallest is three or four inches long and the largest might go twenty inches from nose to tip of tail. Many make dramatic color changes ranging from pale green to dark brown. Their feet have phenomenal holding power; juveniles are frequently seen on damp windowpanes. Their brittle tails are flexible but are not prehensile. Most people consider them pretty, and with intelligent and informed care

The knight anole is a semitropical species and the plants in this terrarium are not, but this is unimportant as long as the lizard has comfortable perches, enough space, and the opportunity to sun himself when desired. Photo by J. Dommers.

Above, *Chamaeleo cristatus*; below, *Chamaeleo chamaeleon.*
Chameleons are agressive animals with large mouths; to call them
charming and affectionate would be stretching the truth. Photo
above by Dr. O. Klee; that below by J. Bridges.

A common green anole, *Anolis carolinensis.* This specimen could have a little more fat at the base of the tail, but it does look healthy. The opening between the eye and the shoulder is the ear. Photo by Van Raam.

they do well in captivity, even to the point of reproducing themselves. They are active when warm and torpid when cold. They do not burrow below the frost line and so are not established where they may be subjected to a hard long frost. Reports of wintering-over or established stable populations in New Jersey or Connecticut should be examined closely. There is the possibility that the wintering actually took place against a protected casement window facing on a basement which was radiating heat all winter. This would be something less than natural "wintering-over."

There are native populations of other species of lizards as far north as southern Canada, but these animals are more terrestrial than arboreal and can burrow deeply to avoid the hard frost. Also they are commonly larger than anoles and so can more efficiently store and expend their stored fats for energy during hibernation. In this manner they don't starve before springtime. The ideal temperature range for the common green anole is probably 75° to 95° F. The animal adjusts its body temperature by moving about within its territory to find the sun or shade it desires.

Population density is governed by food supply and predators. Eventually in ideal conditions it reaches a saturation point when the territories of two individuals overlap by even a silly millimeter. Now real estate and not food rears its ugly head and someone has got to go. Perhaps this is how populations spread. The smallest anole in a crowded cage or a crowded shrub will not grow until the population (and aggression) pressure is relieved, regardless of the food supply. A frightened anole simply will not eat. He will starve with food crawling over his nose if the threatening posture of a larger specimen nearby hovers over him.

With humane and intelligent treatment most anoles become quite tame in captivity and many can be trained to take food from their owner's hand.

Endangered Species

Start with the common green anole, *A. carolinensis*. It is not endangered. It is common. Keep one or two. *Read* this book. Join a herpetological society, attend meetings, learn which species are hardy and common. Keep them. Avoid expensive, rare, delicate forms until you become an expert. A determined, rich fool could easily wipe out all the individuals of any one of several species of lizards known to inhabit just one small island, for example. There is no endangered species of anole or chameleon so desirable that a collector must possess it. For every rare anole there are a dozen common forms, and for most of us the common green anole is the ideal pet from every standpoint —and with intelligent care it may even reproduce itself in captivity.

If beginning pet keepers refuse to purchase rare or endangered species, then collectors and dealers will be less prone to bother with them and perhaps these creatures will be able to retain their place in the sun a little longer.

Some endangered species are imported by unscrupulous dealers who deliberately mis-label the shipments to get through Customs. This serves to make the animal still more endangered and closer to extinction. It also serves to further irritate the more humane among us humans and really aggravates the lunatic fringe—eventually restrictive legislation will make any pet keeping virtually illegal. This is a serious problem which informed pet keepers can control if they are willing to restrain themselves a little.

The Anole's Tail

To escape their enemies, anoles are able to drop parts of their tail. These lost appendages are then regenerated, and the new tail grows out from the stump. There is sometimes some small scar or lump to memorialize the event, and the new tip is not always quite as long as the original. This tail loss happens only infrequently in nature. Observations by this author of *A. carolinensis* suggest that perhaps as few as 10% of the wild adult anoles he has examined ever lost their tails. When a tail grows back, the first few thousand cells are most important; if they are damaged as they grow, the new tail may develop crooked or as a Y or even as a trident.

The tail of the anole is not prehensile and cannot be wrapped around a limb, but it is functional. Anoles are great jumpers and the tail seems to help in maintaining balance. The base of the tail is a storage place for fat. Also, the shape, long and tapering, may help to keep the animal hidden from its enemies since it tends to make the whole lizard look like a tapering twig or a vine. The anole's tail is flexible but it is not a weapon as is that of the iguana. While the common iguana can release part of its tail as a *last* resort, the first use of the tail is as a weapon. To avoid tail loss of captive anoles, avoid handling them. If they must be picked up, let them crawl onto your hand or use a noose or a net; certainly never grasp an anole by its tail.

The common green anole has a perfect tail. It tapers smoothly without kinks or knobs and is somewhat longer than the distance from nose to vent. Photo by the author.

By contrast with anoles, all but perhaps a half dozen of the known chameleons have prehensile tails, and all are tightly fixed. No tail release is possible for chameleons, and loss would be a catastrophe since the tail is like a fifth leg necessary to support the great harpoon of a tongue.

Anoles — Nods, Bobs and Throat Fans

The behavior of the anole is a topic of much research, and many students have climbed the ladder of academic recognition on the back of an anole. This work is often performed by a young graduate student who goes to Puerto Rico, the Virgin Islands, or Costa Rica with his wife for a month or two. They live in a cottage near a colony of anoles and she (the young wife of the graduate student) sits with a pencil, a pad of paper, and a stop watch while he (the graduate student) performs some experiment which causes the anole to distend his throat fan, nod or bob his head, or perform push-ups. Eventually the report is written and published and hopefully the graduate student becomes a psychiatrist or at least a psychologist. Since there are hundreds of kinds of anoles and no one knows if every species nods and bobs and does push-ups the same way, there is plenty of room for additional research of this sort.

Your anole will nod and bob and distend its throat fan. The fan is distended by muscles working on cartilage and bone, not by air, and the result is a tightly stretched thin membrane, usually bright red in the male *A. carolinensis*. In other species the color is sometimes white, yellow, orange or brown. Males display the fan when they

Male and female anoles both have throat fans, but the female never displays hers as much as the male does. This male could expand the fan even more if he wanted to. Photo by the author.

assert themselves to establish territories or perhaps impress females. Females of some species have the equipment necessary but they display their throat fans less frequently and with less gusto. The throat fan is less brightly colored in the female. It is rarely displayed by frightened, sick, or cold specimens; a healthy male might distend his as frequently as a barnyard cock might crow. The exact shape of the throat fan is of some concern to taxonomists since it is a feature which varies in shape, color, and size from species to species.

Anole Reproduction

A common green anole is sexually mature at about one year of age. The adults do not live as pairs, but when a female is mature and receptive there is generally a male nearby to do the honors. The sperm she receives is retained in her body until she is about to lay an egg; at that time the egg is fertilized as it descends the oviduct.

Eggs are laid in damp (not wet) earth, generally described as sandy or gravelly soil. They are also deposited in holes or cracks in rotten moist trees, humus, or damp punky wood. From one to fifteen eggs are laid in a single season, which in northern Florida for instance might begin in April and continue through June. One egg is laid at a time and not in the same spot but perhaps in the same area as other eggs are laid by the same or other female anoles. Eggs are laid one at a time alternately from each of the two ovaries and the interval between eggs may be anywhere from one day up. The average during the egg-laying period is a thirteen-day interval between eggs.

The parents provide no care for eggs or young except that the female does hide or bury them in a moist place away from direct sunlight. Since there is no great effort in hiding eggs or nest building or care, there is no advantage in depositing the eggs all at one time or in putting all the eggs in one spot. The male copulates with the female from time to time and, since she retains viable sperm which then fertilizes the egg as it is about to be laid, there is no need for males to accompany the females during egg-laying. By contrast, a male frog must be right on the spot. The sperm might be retained in the female's body as long as four or five months.

When laid, the eggs of the common green anole weigh about 0.27 grams (about 1/100 of an ounce). After being laid, the eggs absorb moisture and gain weight. A female might weigh 2.7 grams, so each egg represents 10% of her body weight. If she lays fifteen eggs in a season, the total egg weight would be one and a half times her body weight. Obviously this lifestyle would be impossible if she were to lay all her eggs simultaneously "in one basket." For one thing, a predatory, arboreal, and active lizard would find it impossible to carry such a load of eggs and still climb and jump in pursuit of insect prey.

This anole way of life is diametrically opposite that of the chameleons. Here we see slow-moving predators who gather food by rapid extension of their tongues and little else in the way of muscular effort or rapid movement. The female chameleon can and does carry relatively larger eggs or she bears large living young several at a time.

Anole eggs hatch in a month or more depending on species and temperature. Incidentally, all anoles lay eggs and never bear living young. Certain other genera of lizards are live-bearing and still others lay eggs *or* produce living young depending on the environmental conditions. Some species of lizard are even parthenogenetic and unfertilized females produce unfertilized female offspring, generation after generation.

The newly hatched anoles are precocious and resemble their parents. They are self-sufficient and begin to eat tiny insects as soon as they are out of their leathery egg shells. Growth is rapid, and maturity depends on food supply. Semitropical species are fully active all year long, and for them most forms are sexually mature in about a year.

The year-old female common green anole may be sexually active for three or four breeding seasons. She might mate once or several times in the spring and begin to lay eggs immediately and then become sexually inactive after laying perhaps a dozen to fifteen eggs. She would then

Fruitflies (*Drosophila*) are good food for small lizards but are difficult to keep captive if the wings are normal. A vestigial winged mutation is easily available from dealers and cannot fly. Photo by P. Imgrund.

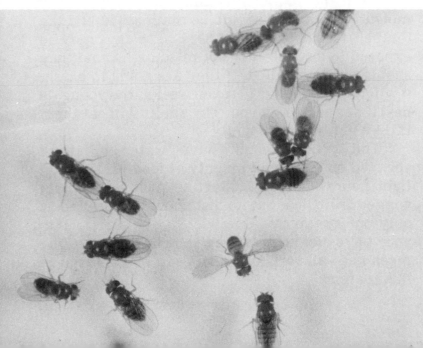

repeat the entire process the following year.

Anoles in captivity are frequently bred and the offspring successfully raised without special equipment or effort. This is one of the rewards of the pet keeping hobby: the satisfaction of keeping a line of life going. There is no other reason for this effort, as there is no economic value to breeding these lizards commercially since they are so common and easily caught.

A female will lay eggs regardless of whether a male is nearby. If she had been fertilized by a male during the previous five months it is possible that the eggs are fertile. She will lay up to fifteen eggs at intervals of one to fifteen days and then will not lay again until the following year.

These leathery eggs should *not* be turned (like hens' eggs in an incubator), but simply placed in moist (not wet) moss, moist sandy earth, moist rotten wood, or moist humus with access to air. They will absorb moisture and gain in weight. The moisture in the soil should be maintained and the temperature held at about 88° F. The eggs may be exposed to daylight but not to sunlight, and they should not be handled. If they are going to hatch, it will happen in four to seven weeks; the young do best if not helped by you. The adults will eat them if they get the opportunity.

The young should have water to drink sprayed on leaves and plenty of food all the daylight hours. One good starting food is vestigial winged fruitflies, but no diet should be limited to only one organism. One way to put variety into your pet's diet is to "sweep" the lawn with a fine mesh net—all sorts of insects will be captured in this manner.

Natural History
of Chameleons

The 80 or so species within the family Chamaeleonidae have many features of structure and behavior in common with all other reptiles, but those which they retain exclusively (or nearly so) are the most spectacular. They share with a few other families the ability to change color, but chameleons do it better. They have their grasping toes arranged in bundles of two on one side and three on the other. They (most of them) have prehensile tails. They operate their eyes independently of each other. They are slow, so slow as to make tortoises appear like hares. They have tongues which in some species extend to their total body plus tail length and are thrown out with the precision of Captain Ahab's harpoon in his battle with Moby Dick. All but one known species are arboreal. All the chameleon species which the author has seen or to which he has found reference are aggressive toward each other and defend their territories vigorously.

Their color changing is legendary. Some species display and control more hues than others, but all do it to some degree. The anoles rival them, but only to rate a rather poor second place. The chameleons' range is from yellow to nearly black, favoring the forest colors of brown and

green; most anoles are limited to browns and greens with red or orange throat fans. Changes can be achieved in just a few minutes and frequently represent changes in disposition rather than an attempt to perfectly match their surroundings.

The mechanism for changing colors is essentially the same for anoles as well and, briefly, it works like this: There are four layers of skin which control color. The layer nearest the outside

The tails of arboreal chameleons are often carried in a coil, but they are hooked around something when the tongue goes into action. Photo of *Chamaeleo cristatus* by Dr. O. Klee.

contains yellow *pigment*, and some scattered red. Under the yellow-red layer is a layer which *reflects* blue. Under the blue reflecting layer is a layer which reflects white. The deepest layer contains a dark brown pigment, and these cells are like mushrooms or stems pushed up through the upper layers.

The outer layer expands or contracts and the bottom layer of brown shifts within the stems. The mixture of colors of the top yellow-red plus the bottom brown and the amount of light which is reflected from the blue and white reflecting surfaces determines the final appearance.

Hormones and state of nervousness (nerve control) determine color in chameleons, but in the anoles experimental data suggest that the color change is purely hormone controlled. This is a problem for physiologists to solve—for the pet keeper, the effect is the same.

Sick lizards tend to be grey.

Healthy lizards tend to be brightly colored brown or green.

Sleeping lizards tend to be pale.

Overheated lizards tend to be pale.

Angry lizards tend to be dark.

Their toes are highly specialized. All but the one terrestrial chameleon have five toes on each foot. These toes are arranged in bundles of two and three. The front feet have three toes outboard and two inboard and the hind feet are arranged in the reverse order. The grasp is surprisingly strong. If you pull a perched chameleon from his twig you may very well break some of his bones or fatally injure him. The anole, by contrast, is flat-footed. He has scales on his feet and toes which tend to hook into the slightest roughness. Anoles have no trouble climbing vertical plastered walls which would completely stymie a chameleon.

Their tails will not come off at the slightest provocation as is the case with anoles. Rather, the chameleon's tail is on to stay permanently. Furthermore, in all but a few dwarf species it is not only strong but prehensile. This gives the chameleon a five-point contact with his perch. Visualize a gun platform that is mobile, equipped with binocular vision, camouflage, and a projectile both massive and sticky. The tail is an integral part of the system and holds on like grim death. The chameleon's tail is muscular and at its base may be quite stout—partly muscle and partly stored fat, a reserve against hard times or the burden of producing eggs or living young.

Their eyes are like no other eyes in the chordate phylum. They are mounted in conical drums and are manipulated singly or in concert to focus on targets as small as a pinhead perhaps ten inches away. The opening of the eye is but a tiny spot in the scaly drum swinging about in search of enemy or prey.

When a fly settles on a twig perhaps a scant foot in front of a chameleon, one or perhaps both eyes will focus on it, the mouth will open a trifle, and the tongue will stick out an inch or two or three, as if taking aim. Suddenly, and too fast for the human eye to catch the action, the fly is gone and the tongue is gone and the chameleon is chewing.

The chameleon has binocular vision—he can see the same spot with both eyes and thereby guage distances, but he is not dependent on this ability to survive. Experiments have shown that with one eye covered over, the batting average remains the same—better than the proverbial 300—but the productivity (times at bat) drops off somewhat.

Their slowness is something you must witness to believe. The only rapid movement is from the tongue. Even the eyes swivel slowly—the legs and tail move even slower. They fight slowly. Two horned chameleons battling for a choice twig in a choice territory might take five minutes getting into position and another five minutes could then go by before one asserted his dominance over the other. Then still another five minutes might expire before the vanquished retired from the battlefield.

Since they capture their prey through stealth and avoid predators through camouflage, there is no need for speed. Speed would defeat the purpose which all the chameleon's other attributes combine to achieve. Try to catch a fly with your fingers and you will soon discover a critical speed. Move slower than this speed and the fly will not buzz off. This is the chameleon's secret.

Chameleon food includes grasshoppers, locusts, and crickets, and these three insects are all capable of high velocity jumps with instant take-offs. A running attack would never be fast enough. Another thought about chameleon feeding is that many of these Old World lizards are found in thorny plants. A jump would put them in jeopardy of impalement.

The slow movement of chameleons is sufficient for finding food since the food comes to the animal. This way of life presents new problems and new solutions. Problems include predators and territorial rights. The thorns take care of most predators. Protective coloration helps too, and so does the large mouth with a brightly colored interior for defense of territory. The teeth are not much use for defense, but the large mouth and hissing noises may help. The chameleon also puffs himself up with air and appears much larger under certain conditions of stress. This might help to discourage smaller enemies and is another possible solution in the battle for survival.

The slowness of African chameleons is legendary, and for this book one example should suf-

Chamaeleo pumila, one of the small chameleons formerly placed in *Microsaura.* Photo by Muller-Schmida.

fice. In Rhodesia today there are people who call the chameleon "Go-Slowly" and attach to it a legend which goes to "Back in the Beginning" when "He Whose Name is Not Spoken" made all men alike and put them on earth. Then, after a while, He was dissatisfied with the results of His efforts. So He decided to bring all men together again and improve them. He would give each group special attributes. He sent animals out as messengers, and to various tribes of men He sent various species of animals. Now in those days the chameleons were not at all slow, but rather they traveled at reasonable rates of speed. A chameleon was chosen to go to the people of Rhodesia, but he dragged his feet and by the time the order to assemble was delivered and the Rhodesians arrived to receive their special attributes, the most desirable had already been assigned. The wretched Rhodesians felt cheated and put a curse on the chameleon. Henceforth all chameleons would go slowly. The myth is still believed by some people and to this day they fear that the chameleon will try to get revenge on *his* oppressor. So it is a good policy to avoid (or kill) any chameleon to protect oneself against a horrible vengeance.

Their tongues are unique in the animal kingdom. No other lizard, reptile, or any other creature is endowed with a tongue which even resembles the tongue of a chameleon. A close second are the toads and the frogs which can throw out their sticky tongues a distance about equal to the length of their heads. Some chameleon species can impale a fly at a distance about equal to their total length, tail included! Robert Cushman Murphy of the American Museum of Natural History mentions a chameleon with a seven-inch *body length* which captured a fly twelve inches away.

The mechanism of the tongue is well known. It has been formally studied since 1805, and in 1937 a bibliography and text was published in *Proceedings of the Zoological Society of London* (Volume 107, pages 1-63); the author was Dr. C.P. Gnanamuthu. The back of the tongue is fastened to the bones of the lower jaw. The essential components are the tube-like tongue itself with its lump of a sticky tip, a slippery bone spike on which the tube is retracted, and a muscular, ring-like structure which works somewhat like a small boy manipulating a slippery watermelon seed between his fingers at a Labor Day picnic. The ring muscle contracts and drives the sticky tip forward off the point of the bony spike—and on it goes until it strikes something solid or extends full length. The muscle relaxes and the tube-like tongue snaps back generally with a stuck and sometimes stunned insect attached. Large specimens of large species can and do catch mice and small birds with this tremendous harpoon.

Anoles have sticky tongues but their claim to fame is agility and rapid movements. Anoles are prone to sneak up and then jump with an open mouth. They literally leap upon their prey.

Their territoriality is a big thing in their lives. This is true for chameleons and also anoles. They spend a good part of the daylight hours defending or extending their domains. This is sometimes accomplished among anoles with their nodding, bobbing, push-ups, and throat fan displays. Sometimes they bite each other. Chameleons are more deliberate, more assertive, and meaner. They open their large mouths, hiss, inhale air, and inflate their bodies (to look larger?); they poke each other with their heads or horns if so blessed, and they bite if the opportunity presents itself. This takes a lot of energy and probably creates a lot of stress. Perhaps this constant acrimony contributes to short lives. If you keep more than one anole or one chameleon in a cage, it should be a big cage with plenty of good hiding places and desirable perches.

Their puffing, hissing, and general meanness is mostly directed at their own species. This is a trait which behaviorists may well examine in more detail. Is it necessary for survival that they be so mean to each other? Does fighting improve their aim or make the sticky saliva accumulate on their tongues? Is this a sexually inspired trait or is it universal among all animals but just more spectacular among chameleons?

Chameleon Reproduction

As is also true among some other families of lizards, some species of chameleons give birth to living young and others lay eggs. The live-bearers are generally considered to be ovoviviparous. The egg is retained within the female's body but is not

Juvenile chameleons more closely resemble the female than the male at birth. If the species has male specializations such as horns, these will appear with growth. Photo by Muller-Schmida.

nourished during its development. The young are born as exact but tiny counterparts of their parents. Sexual differences in size, scales, and facial flaps and horns (where present) all come after maturity. Species which lay eggs bury them in moist sand. This is a seasonal thing in most of their range, as holes cannot be dug during the wet season (they would flood) or during the dry season (the ground is too hard and furthermore the eggs would dry out).

It is possible that the live-bearers evolved because there was no good season for placement of eggs in the ground. Chameleons do not take care of the eggs or the young but simply dig a tunnel and deposit their eggs in a cavity and plug up the entrance. This is a rather tedious job for an animal which is virtually a cripple on land and is hardly more suited to digging holes than to opening coconuts. Eggs, once laid, take as long as 170 (or even more) days to hatch.

Chameleons in Captivity

The author kept a dozen adult *Chamaeleo jacksoni* in a heated cage some years ago. They were all dead in eight months. They did eat well, mostly on crickets and mealworms, and they drank a lot of water. The last survivors (obviously) lived the longest, but actually when there was only one in the cage it lived several months after

Adult male Jackson's chameleon, *Chamaeleo jacksoni*. Photo by Muller-Schmida.

the previous one died. This observation coupled with a search of the literature suggests several aspects to the problem of keeping chameleons alive for long periods in captivity.

To start out, there is no mass of solid evidence to tell us how long they live in the wild. Granted, most chameleons born in captivity die before maturity. This suggests we are doing something wrong. Perhaps we could assume an average life for an average chameleon to be five years and then aim at that as we care for them.

The observation that the last survivor in the cage lasted much longer than its cagemate has also been made by others, and it tells us that chameleons don't get along with each other. Species should be kept apart and individuals should be given territories which do not overlap. These animals move slowly and seem to be very jealous of the areas they stake out for themselves.

Chameleons do not readily drink from dishes, but they assuredly need much more moisture than they get from the insects they eat. Some of this moisture may be absorbed through their skins—in nature it is reasonable to expect much dew in arid tropical mountainous regions where daytime temperatures reach 90° and nights are as cool as 40° F. To get dew in a cage is easy. It can be sprayed in at night or early morning. To dry it out daily is also easy; incandescent lights will cause evaporation during the day. Humid cage atmospheres for extended periods are known to bring disease, usually skin fungus on reptiles like chameleons.

Dew notwithstanding, most chameleons in captivity seem eternally thirsty, and a dripping watering device should be provided. If you have more than one chameleon in the cage, be sure that *all* the animals get enough to drink.

Food in large *quantity* and *variety* is critical. Live crickets, grasshoppers, flies, spiders, and perhaps even caterpillars should be offered. Giant chameleons will eat mice and small birds. Juveniles often start out in captivity with fruit-flies and mealworms, but this may be too much roughage and some softer bodied food like spiders should be offered, too. Mealworms are sometimes soft and always nourishing, but again the pet keeper should not fall into the rut of offering just mealworms. We already know that it doesn't fill the bill-of-fare adequately.

Incidentally, crickets are available anywhere in the U.S. nearly twelve months of the year from dealers in fish bait. Advertisements are found in the sport fishing and hunting magazines. Crickets are relatively inexpensive and easy to keep alive until feeding time. It is easier to buy them than to breed them. One small problem is that they tend to escape, and they eat some types of fiber rugs. One small adult chameleon can easily polish off five crickets a day, and large giant chameleons have eaten as many as twenty crickets per day.

Do not assume that because a female chameleon gives birth or lays eggs in captivity you have mastered the breeding of chameleons in captivity. This much happens frequently, but to raise the babies and have them reproduce themselves is another matter entirely. After success with one species, remember there are 79 or so yet to go.

Catching and Housing Lizards

Anoles and chameleons are alike in that they sleep at night. This makes nighttime captures for anoles the recommended technique. For chameleons the situation is complicated by the nighttime presence of leopards, lions, and the like.

For anoles, a sheet is spread under a shrub or low tree known to be used by anoles. The limbs are then shaken violently and the sleepy anoles simply fall onto the sheet where they are easily seen and picked up. A fishing pole with a six-pound test monofilament noose is also effective for capturing anoles.

Chameleons are hunted by flashlight and must be gently "peeled" from twigs which they grasp with four feet plus the tail. The twigs may also be clipped free from the shrub and the whole "assembly" placed into a bag or carton.

Many pet keepers prefer not to handle their specimens because of the tail-dropping proclivity of some and also the possibility of transmitting diseases from one to another via the handler. For anoles an aquarist's fish net, larger than the specimen, and a piece of cardboard to cover the opening in the net after capture are about all that is required. Captures are easier at night since anoles are active only when they have been exposed to light.

A chameleon can be picked up by gently and slowly pushing a twig between its belly and the thing it is holding on to. Soon it will be on the twig and can be carried about in this manner.

An anole or a chameleon loose in a room is not dangerous and poses no threat to anyone. In many Central American and Florida homes they are encouraged, as are geckos, as beautiful and amusing insect controls. To catch one in summertime use a net at night or a noose in the daytime. Turn on the lights only long enough to find the animal and then stalk it in semidarkness. In cooler climes one trick is to open a window and benumb the little fellow. Then he can be picked up easily—per-

Chamaeleo melleri is constructed somewhat like a very large, toothed leaf and enjoys camouflage of both color and form. Photo by G. Marcuse.

haps he will even crawl into a warm hand for the comfort it affords.

Anoles and chameleons do well if loose in the home or greenhouse and will generally settle on some potted plant in a sunny room. The problem is to be sure your pet gets enough to eat and drink and that you don't inadvertently kill it from a treatment of insecticide. The No-pest® strips are safe with iguanas, but at this writing the author does not know for certain if chameleons and anoles can tolerate them. This, like all poisons, is probably a matter of degree.

Cages should be roomy—the bigger the better. These creatures are strong for territories and they will defend them to the point of killing or demoralizing their rivals. The nearer a cage resembles the natural habitat of its resident, the better off the resident will be. Bear in mind that in many Central American rainforests it rains every day for perhaps eight or more months of the year, and anoles get all the moisture they need for drinking and for aiding in molting. Also bear in mind that it is sunny nearly every day and the lizards have an opportunity to dry thoroughly. To do less will lead to fungus diseases of the skin.

The same problems obtain with the chameleons. They need water and get it from dew condensed by cold nights and warm days. They also need direct warming, drying rays of sunlight. It may be that another key (after water, food and cool nights) is direct sunlight. Chameleons may generate their needed Vitamin D only when they have an opportunity to expose themselves to the direct rays of the sun. An ultraviolet ray lamp for perhaps a half hour daily might suffice as a substitute. Be sure in any case to give the animals an opportunity to crawl out of the light if they wish.

Choose tough plants for your chameleon or anole cage and be sure to include large twigs and sticks with plenty of branches. An all-glass aquarium makes a fine container, but be sure the screen cover is strong enough to keep cats and kids out and lizards in. Photos on this and the facing page by the author.

Housing

Captive small reptiles do well in glass containers with screen covers. The best, least expensive, most reliable, and easiest to clean home for small lizard pets is an all-glass aquarium. If you cannot afford a new tank, buy one with a small crack. Patch the crack with aquarium silicone cement and build a screen cover which fits tightly around the edges. The cover should keep lizards in and keep children, other pets and insects (like botflies) out. Copper or aluminum screen is excellent. Just be sure the screen frame fits snugly. The size of the cage is up to you—the bigger the better of course, but if you wish to keep more than one species or even several specimens of the same species, you might be better off with several smaller cages instead of one big "community" cage. Then if disease strikes you can isolate an animal while you attempt a cure. Also there is the territory problem—many small lizards do better if they are not irritated by neighbors who are a little too close. Each lizard seems to want his own little tract with no trespassing permitted.

Other aspects of caging are the problems of parasites and viewing your specimen. Both these considerations suggest a simple "open" set-up. Don't build caves or forest glens into which your pets will retire and remain forever unseen. One multiforked limb of well dried apple or maple will be much better for both hygiene and viewing than a forest of philodendron. You must compromise between the verdant and impenetrable jungle and the four bare walls of an empty aquarium.

One thing you *must* provide is assurance of shade somewhere in the cage at all times. Your pet must be able to find a way to get into warm sunlight or its equivalent and then out of it again whenever he wishes.

A water *dish* is not too important since most anoles and chameleons will not drink from it anyway. Some fanciers do have good luck with a drip device. These are usually an inverted bottle of water with a capillary tube which accumulates a drop and then holds it until an animal licks it off. Remember, they *must* have water, and plenty of it; the problem is that most of them will not drink from a dish.

Foods for Anoles and Chameleons

Anoles drink water and eat large quantities of live insects. How much? A six-inch anole in a sun-drenched dry cage might consume as much as a quarter to a half teaspoon of water a day. He might refuse to drink from a dish but would spend literally hours licking the dark corner of his aquarium cage where droplets of water have condensed. He should have his cage sprayed daily or at least every other day to provide these droplets of water. Bear in mind that he must also be permitted to dry out thoroughly or skin fungus diseases will result.

This same anole might eat a dozen fruitflies and a small cricket, a cricket and a few moths, or a few tiny crickets or spiders every day. Six really small mealworms might be a decent meal for an eight-inch anole. The larger the animal, the more it will consume. Also, larger specimens favor larger prey. An eight-inch anole would be picking crumbs if all he was offered was "wingless" fruitflies. An animal this large would eat large moths, butterflies, small crickets, mealworms, grubs, houseflies, housefly larvae, and in a pinch small bits of meat and soft fruits such as banana offered from the end of a toothpick. Large specimens of the larger species of anoles are known to eat small mice and small birds, while newborn *A. carolinensis* would eat just spiders, aphids, fruitflies, mosquitoes, and newly hatched and freshly molted mealworms. A steady diet of mealworms is not good for any reptile pet, but as part of a "mixed grill" mealworms are great. An excellent book describing the methods of capturing and rearing live foods for animal pets is *Live Foods for the Aquarium and Terrarium* by Willy Jocher (TFH Publications, Neptune, New Jersey, 1973).

In Florida the native *A. carolinensis* is no longer the only species. Key West, Miami, Coral Gables, Tampa, and St. Petersburg all have populations of "exotics" which arrived via banana boats or small boys. One such importation is established in Coral Gables and is described by Vincent Brach in a short article entitled "Habits and food of *Anolis equestris* in Florida," *Copeia*, 1976, No. 1: 187-189. The diet of this lizard, commonly

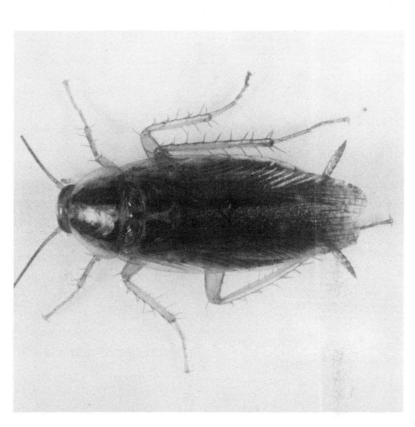

Cockroaches are fine food for large anoles and chameleons. They can be trapped or bred in carefully closed containers. Never use cockroaches (or any other insect for that matter) from an area which has been sprayed with any insecticide less than two weeks earlier. Photo by P. Imgrund.

called the Cuban knight anole, is documented from analysis of stomach contents, and it is absolutely clear that this species, at least, naturally eats the fruits of the Bo tree (*Ficus religiosa*) in addition to the moths, grasshoppers, crickets, spiders, and cockroaches we already know about. There is no evidence to suggest preference of food, simply that these anoles do eat some fruit. Territoriality and display are also described in this excellent paper.

It is easy to make a small *temporary* home for a chameleon. The materials required are a clean jar, gravel, artificial plants, a small rock, a hammer, a nail or punch, and some imagination. Holes must be made in the jar cap for air. But remember that a setup like this is only temporary; it is cruel to keep the animal in such cramped quarters for more than a day or so.

The materials shown on the opposite page have been assembled and a little water and food dish have been added, along with (of course) a chameleon. It must be pointed out that this is not a truly adequate environment; roomier arrangements are available at all pet shops at relatively low cost. Such arrangements offer much more leeway for decorating the chameleon's home and also are much easier to clean.

Diseases

An anole might live three to five years in the wild or in captivity before succumbing to old age. The longevity of chameleons in the wild is not well established, nor is it particularly long in captivity. Two years in captivity seems to be the upper limit. During their lives in captivity these lizards suffer from thirst, malnutrition, overheating, underheating, damp induced fungus diseases, parasites, and various internal bacterial disorders. The first five items above have been considered elsewhere in this book, so let's begin with parasites.

These include botflies, mites, and ticks externally, and worms internally. Ticks (there are many species) resemble the ticks found on dogs, cats and sometimes on ourselves. They move slowly, resemble short-legged spiders, come in various colors, and suck blood from living animals. They are sometimes found on recently acquired pet lizards, but once removed and killed they rarely reappear. Examine any lump on your pet with a magnifying glass. A tick full of blood will be so fat as to hide its legs in its own bulk. Then it might be any size from a pinhead to a small pea. The ticks on a recently acquired pet are probably a tropical form and will not establish themselves outside their natural habitat.

Pick ticks off your pet with tweezers. Perhaps lemon juice, vinegar, alcohol, or tobacco juice helps, but generally a slow gentle tug will suffice. Sometimes when a tick is pulled off part of his head remains embedded in his host's skin. Generally it is cast off in a scab or during molting and that is the end of it. If the area seems irritated you might apply a tiny dab of an antibiotic cream or simply wipe the area with an alcohol swab.

Mites are so small that most people cannot see them without magnification, but they, like ticks, suck blood and should be eliminated. Sometimes when you don't see a mite you do see a fine dust of his white or pale grey droppings on your pet. They may appear in just one area around the neck or head or at the base of the tail, perhaps. Mites are too small to be picked off with tweezers, but the control is not much of a chore. First, you should have a sterilized cage to put your pets into after you treat them. To do less would be a waste of time. If you are about to eliminate mites, plan ahead and get the cage cleaned at the same time. Mites can be roasted, dried, drowned, or poisoned. Proceed as follows:

1) Remove the animals from their cage and place them in clean, dry, bare quarters—an empty aquarium is great.

2) Sterilize the bark, twigs, rocks, gravel, food dishes, screen cover, and the entire cage or whatever you house them in. Wash with hot water, rinse and dry thoroughly—a hot sunny day helps. Bake the gravel, scorch the wood, scrub the dishes—be thorough.

3A) Treat the animals with a total immersion in cage-temperature water; soak them (but avoid drowning them) for a few minutes. The mites will probably float away or drown. Put your pet back in his sterilized cage and hopefully you have elim-

An aqua-terrarium arrangement allows chameleons to live on the dry part with small amphibians or fish in the water. In the close-up at left, you can see the effect of the chameleon's natural camouflage. Photos by Richard Haas.

The natural surroundings of a woodland terrarium make the chameleon feel at home. Photo by Van Den Nieuwenhuizen.

The matching of this male's color to its background is coincidental. Photo by Richard Haas.

inated the mites. Certainly you have reduced the infestation. Some eggs may survive to hatch out later, so a second treatment may be necessary.

3B) If 3A did not work, try No. 1 and No. 2 again and then apply Sulphanone, an insecticide. This is harmless to reptiles but death on mites. Your pet dealer or perhaps your veterinarian can sell you some. Two dollars worth should last you a lifetime unless you are a zoo curator. The Sulphanone should be dusted on and left for 18 hours, then washed off with several rinses, each rinse in fresh water, at room temperature.

3C) If you cannot get the Sulphanone readily, try a brushing or swabbing with a mixture of 90% grain alcohol and castor oil. The proportions are equal volumes of the two ingredients. This also works for mites on your chickens' scaly feet if you have some left over. Don't dip your pet—you will intoxicate or dehydrate him if you do more than apply a little with a cotton swab. Remember that 90% grain alcohol is not 90 proof but is in fact twice as strong. You can buy a bottle in a liquor store and use the remainder any way you see fit. A little goes a long way.

3D) If 3A or 3B or 3C doesn't work or is not convenient, then as a last resort try a plastic insecticide strip or a piece of your dog's flea collar in the cage for one week per month until the situation is under control.

CAUTION — Do *not* use DDT or related insecticide poisons in any spray or powder in or around reptiles; even a small dose is often fatal to the host.

There are also internal parasites. These are worms much like the worms which infest dogs and cats and even people who walk barefoot in warm places. The trouble with parasitic worms in tiny reptiles is that you probably will not know that your pet is endangered until it is practically dead. The only saving grace here is that the ideal parasites lives with a *host*, not a *victim*. The parasite is left homeless if his host should die. The next small ray of sunshine in this vale of tears is that many parasitic worms go through life cycles which require a second host—another totally different animal. Examples of this exist throughout nature. Witness the worm which lives out part of his cycle in a fish where he eventually encysts himself. Then a bird eats the fish and another stage of the cycle of the parasite takes place in the intestinal cavity of the bird. The worm eggs eventually get back into the fish pond when the bird defecates over the water and the cycle repeats itself. The same goes for many internal parasites of reptiles, so if you keep your pets isolated from other animals and insects you will go a long way toward naturally eliminating the problem.

If you are planning to visit a veterinarian with a problem, remember that the veterinarian is a professional who earns his living treating animals to improve their health. If he is called upon to spend an hour diagnosing or treating the disease of your lizard he is entitled to be paid as much as if he spent an hour setting a broken bone in a dog's leg.

If you made the mistake of obtaining your pet from a cageful of sunken-eyed, emaciated, grey, thin-tailed snufflers, then you have a problem. It is a problem you should have left in the pet shop. Eventually that pet dealer will straighten up or go broke, but in the meantime here is what you should do:

This *Anolis sagrei* has decided to explore a new addition to its woodland terrarium. Photo by John Dommers.

Molting, or the shedding of skin, is natural. A light spraying of water every day will be helpful during molting.

1) Isolate any new acquisition.

2) Feed your pet as much as it will eat.

3) Try a penicillin type drug if the lizard seems sick.

4) Provide sunlight—preferably direct and unfiltered.

5) Keep temperatures higher than normal—say 82° to 90° F.

6) Keep the cage clean and dry—really clean—antiseptically clean—"Lysol" clean. Be sure the antiseptic is thoroughly and completely rinsed out and the cage is bone-dry before re-introducing

Molting in lizards is sometimes incomplete and small patches of old skin may remain. In the anole pictured here the skin seems to be peeling off in one piece with no help from the keeper. If there is a minor problem with the molt, a fine spray of luke-warm water some-times helps. Photo by the author.

the sick specimen. Keep the "hospital" cage simple to avoid places where germs and parasites can remain undetected.

Sometimes a small lizard will be found to be suffering from a mouth infection commonly called mouth rot. This infectious disease attacks run-down animals who suffered mouth injuries. The problem is exacerbated when the animal cannot eat because his mouth is sore, and so he also starves. Symptoms are yellow patches, cottony substances, and yellow crust on jaws and gums. You will need help from your veterinarian on this one since the treatment requires a prescription antibiotic like penicillin ointment rubbed on the infected areas and more penicillin administered orally or injected.

Don't plan to clip your pet's toenails or otherwise groom him—you will surely do more harm than good. If a small lizard has trouble with his molting you might be sure to spray him every day with pure plain room temperature tap water. Don't keep him wet, just a daily spraying in an otherwise dry cage.

Another problem is the botfly—the adult lays her egg on the lizard (usually in a wound) and the maggot digs under the skin to mature. Getting at a botfly maggot is surgery best left to a professional. Experiment on a dead lizard if the occasion arises. If your cage has a fine mesh screen this is not a problem.

Chamaeleo jacksoni, looking more fierce in this close-up than it actually is. Photo by Karl Alexander.

Opposite, bottom: *Anolis carolinensis.*
Photo by G. Marcuse. **Opposite, top:**
Anolis gundlachi. Photo by S. Minton.

Immigrant Anoles

Mainland U.S.A. has but one native species, *Anolis carolinensis carolinensis*. Perhaps it is more properly a binomial rather than a trinomial (another subspecies is in the Bahamas), but let's not quibble about that. This is the common green anole sold in pet shops and carnivals all over North America. Sometimes it is green and sometimes it changes its color to brown. The male displays a red or pink throat fan. It grows to a total length of perhaps 7½ inches, and most uninformed people call it "a chameleon." The Florida Keys, especially Key West, have another anole which may be native to these islands but not to the mainland. The common name of this one is Key West anole, and scientifically it has been called *Anolis sagrei stejnegeri*. Some authorities are not fully in agreement and suggest that it is a race and not a valid subspecies. Regardless, it *is* a genuine *Anolis* and it varies its colors through several shades of yellow specked brown, but never green. When viewed from below the male displays a light or white streak longitudinally along its throat. This stripe becomes the white border of a brilliant orange-red throat fan when he displays it. Now, thanks to small boys this island form is found on the mainland as well.

To make matters worse, some authorities have found that the Cuban brown anole, *Anolis sagrei sagrei*, and the Bahaman brown anole, *A.s.*

This large knight anole is trying, unsuccessfully, to climb a pane of glass. Because of the toe pads an anole can climb almost smooth vertical surfaces, but the large sizes and relatively great weight of some species limit their climbing ability. This particular knight anole is too thin for comfort, the legs being especially emaciated and little fat stored in the base of the tail. Photo by G. Marcuse.

Anolis equestris with throat fan distended is shown above, to be compared with specimen on opposite page. Both photos by G. Marcuse.

ordinatus, are also established on mainland Florida. If once they get to Disneyworld, they will soon be everywhere. The positive identification of these three races or subspecies is not properly part of this book but is a subject for highly trained specialists.

Still another immigrant to mainland U.S. is the Bahaman bark anole, sometimes called the yellow throated anolis, *Anolis distichus*. It is never longer than 4½ inches overall and varies in color from pale grey to dark brown. The male displays a pale yellow throat fan and both sexes have faint V-shaped marks on their backs. A straight dark line connects the eyes. The diet and care is about the same for all. Spiders, fruitflies, houseflies, crickets, small grasshoppers, and sometimes a piece of fresh ripe fruit with droplets of water always available seem to suffice for all these small tree-dwelling lizards. More about what they eat may be learned through the index. This immigrant from the Bahamas is considered by some as a distinct subspecies, *A.d. floridanus*. But wait! We are still going strong—there is also in Florida at least one established colony of green bark anoles. The source of this species is Haiti and the Dominican Republic, where it is technically known as *Anolis distichus dominicensis*. Maximum length seems to be about five inches, and colors vary from mottled greenish grey to reddish or yellowish brown.

The largest anole immigrant to date is the knight anole, also sometimes called the giant Cuban anole, *Anolis equestris*. This species, found now in southern Florida, is of Cuban origin and is much larger than most of its near relatives. Total lengths may reach twenty inches; when they are that large they can (and do) eat smaller lizards, mice, small birds, and virtually all large insects. John Dommers found that his eleven-inch male ignored crickets but avidly ate grasshoppers. If one is kept as a pet in northern climes, substitute food would be in order for winter. Perhaps the food which the crickets had been eating gave them a less than appetizing odor. Other pet keepers have found that their knight anoles will eat some species of caterpillars, strips of raw fat-free beef heart, parts of road-killed birds, and newborn or very small mice in addition to roaches and other large insects.

Still another immigrant to our shores is the Haitian anole, *Anolis cybotes cybotes*. This species is found in southern Florida and seems to favor areas where people live. The maximum size is about eight inches, but the lizard seems much larger because of its broad and blunt head. The colors are not outstanding but vary through shades of tan and brown. The throat fan on the male is reported to be cream, yellow, or peach.

Small isolated colonies of still other immigrant species of the genus *Anolis* are certainly established in the wilderness of the Everglades and may eventually show up in the dealers' lists. While in Florida in 1976 doing research for this book, the author and his daughter Nancy visited The Shed, a Miami reptile dealer, and were shown several handsome pale green large Jamaican anoles which, we were told, had recently been caught by collectors in southern Florida. Not much was known about them then, except that since several sizes were on display we might assume that the colony is established and is reproducing itself.

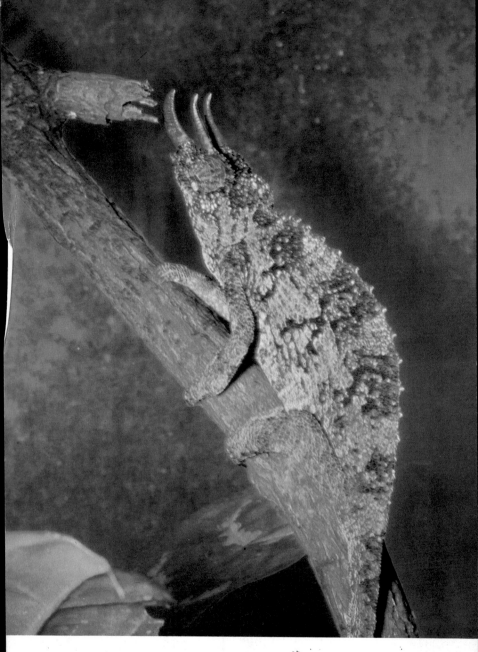

Chamaeleo jacksoni. Note where the legs are attached to the body as well as the differences between fore and hind legs.

Chamaeleo chamaeleon, a slow-moving master of disguise. Photo by Carl Knaack.

Chamaeleo dilepsis, with excellent view of curled tail. Photo by G. Marcuse.

References

For chameleons the best way to get started is with a bibliography, and the one to get started with is *Bibliography of the Chameleontidae, 1864-1964,* by Stephen D. Busack. This paper is available at a reasonable price from the Smithsonian Herpetological Information Services and may be obtained by writing to the Division of Reptiles and Amphibians, U.S. National Museum, Washington, D.C. 20560. There are 520 referenced articles, and many of them are in English. There is probably no library in the United States with all of these documents on file, but with dogged perseverance perhaps all or most could be found somewhere. One article from Busack's list of special interest to pet keepers is entitled "Chamaeleons in Captivity" by Robert Bustard; it appeared in the *British Journal of Herpetology,* Volume 2, No. 9, December 1959, pages 163-165. Although few U.S. public libraries would take or keep this publication, your local librarian can direct you to one of the larger natural history libraries where photocopy service is available.

When it comes to anoles, one of the most comprehensive species lists is by Thomas Barbour. In Volume 70(3) of the 1930 *Bulletin* of the Museum of Comparative Zoology of Harvard College, Cambridge, Massachusetts, pages 105 through 144, he lists the island species; in 1934, Volume 77(4), pages 121 through 155, he covers the mainland species. This is where a herpetologist could start looking to identify a specimen.

Pet keepers who wish to learn more from the experience of others on a continuing basis should become members of a society. These memberships provide an opportunity to publish data and observations in the journals, attend meetings, and to know that membership supports worthwhile scientific study. There are several active state associations of herpetologists and the following national associations:

American Society of Ichthyologists and Herpetologists. Annual meetings and a quarterly journal devoted to cold-blooded vertebrates (*Copeia*). C/O A.S.I.H., Division of Reptiles, U.S. National Museum, Washington, D.C. 20560.

Herpetologists League. Annual meeting and quarterly journal devoted to reptiles and amphibians. C/O H.A. Dundee, Dept. of Zoology, Tulane University, New Orleans, La. 70118.

Society for the Study of Amphibians and Reptiles. Three publications including facsimile reprints. C/O Henri C. Seibert, Dept. of Zoology, Ohio University, Athens, Ohio 45701.

HISS Yearbook of Herpetology, published by the Herpetological Information Search Systems, C/O American Museum of Natural History, New York, N.Y. 10024. The publication lists, for example, chromosome data for 37 chameleons and 77 anoles and the names and addresses of some 3000 herpetologists from all over the world.

With a little patience a chameleon will learn to eat meat from the tip of a straw. The trick is to jiggle it just slightly in order to interest the lizard. After stalking its prey (much as a cat would do), the chameleon seizes the meat with a quick darting motion.

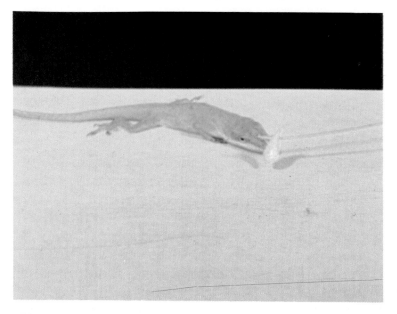

A female chameleon is shown above in her natural habitat. The color of the chameleon blends in with the stems and leaves of the plant. Pictured below is a woodland terrarium constructed for chameleons. Photos by Richard Haas.

The knight anole, *Anolis equestris*, is a recent immigrant to Florida. It is large enough to eat small birds and mice. Notice the wide toe disks; many smaller anoles can actually climb wet windows. Photo by G. Marcuse.

INDEX

Page numbers in *italics* refer to illustrations.